Around The World
HANDWRITING
WORKBOOK

Take a journey around the world while improving handwriting skills.

Around the Word English Alphabet and Handwriting Booklet

Author: C. Nicole Hill

Around the Word English Alphabet and Handwriting Booklet
Copyright © 2021 by C. Nicole Hill

All rights reserved. Published by

Blue Café Books
www.carladupont.com
Atlanta, GA

Printed in the USA.

ISBN: 978-0-578-33157-7

Credits
Editorial: Carla DuPont
Cover Design: Garrett Myers
Interior Design: C. Nicole Hill

This book is dedicated to my wonderful son and angel,
Davis Coleman Smith. You inspire me to do and be
a better human each day.
I love you eternally.

- Mommy

Instructions

Get your imagination ready for a fun and educational trip! This book will teach your child how to write each letter of the alphabet while introducing them to various countries around the world. Each letter is represented by a different country. In this book, your child will practice writing both upper and lower case letters, be able to color, and learn fun facts about each country. Here are three tips you should know before getting started:

 Each section begins with a fun fact coloring page for that letter's country. Example: A is for Australia.

 The next page will present upper and lower case letters for your child to practice tracing each letter.

 The next two pages are for your child to continue writing the upper and lower case letters multiple times.

Bonus: To make this fun learning experience even better, we encourage you and your child to lookup the countries' flags as you go and color each flag appropriately. No matter what, just have fun and enjoy learning!

Australia

Australia is located in the Pacific Ocean and is the sixth largest country in the world. The land is both a continent and country. Australia's capitol city is Canberra and the Australian people speak English. Australia is known as the land of kangaroos and for its famous Sydney Opera House.

Kangaroo

Sydney Opera House

Australia

National Flag

Aa

A is for Australia.

Directions: Practice writing each letter in the spaces provided.

3

Directions: Practice writing the letter in each space provided.

A A A A A

Directions: Practice writing the letter in each space provided.

a a a a a

5

Brazil

Brazil is the largest country in South America. The capital city of Brazil is Brasília and the people of Brazil speak Portuguese. The country's national animal is the jaguar and soccer is a popular sport played by both children and adults.

Soccer Ball

Brazil

National Flag

Jaguar

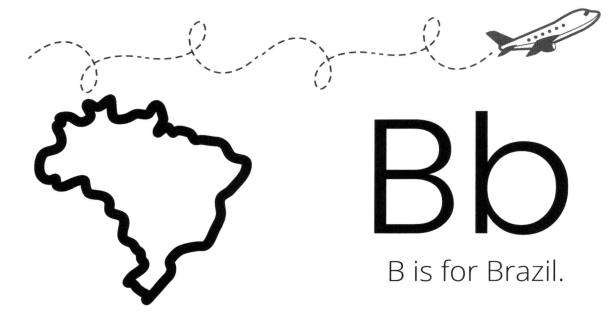

Bb

B is for Brazil.

Directions: Practice writing each letter in the spaces provided.

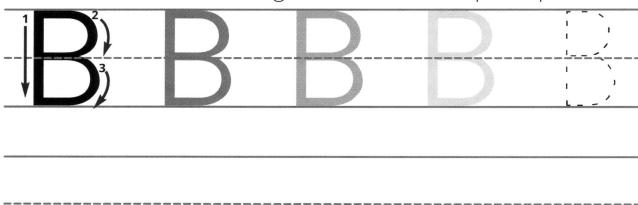

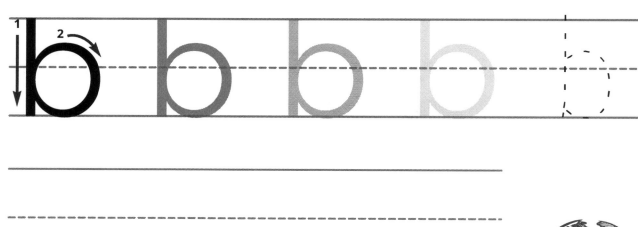

7

Directions: Practice writing the letter in each space provided.

B B B B B

Directions: Practice writing the letter in each space provided.

b b b b b

China

China is the second largest country in Asia; but, has the largest population with 1.4 billion people. Many languages are spoken in China, but Mandarin and Standard Chinese are the official languages. Beijing is the capitol city. This land is home to the world-famous Great Wall of China and the county's national animal is the giant panda.

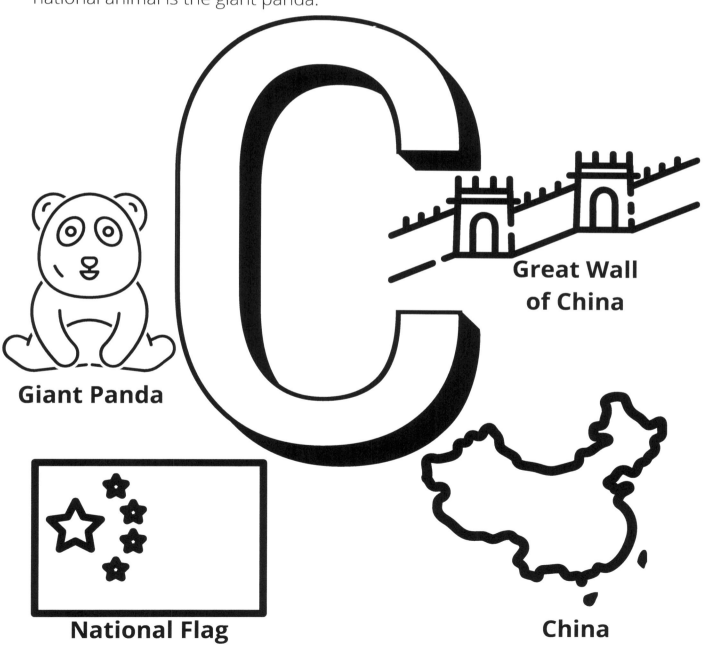

Giant Panda

Great Wall of China

National Flag

China

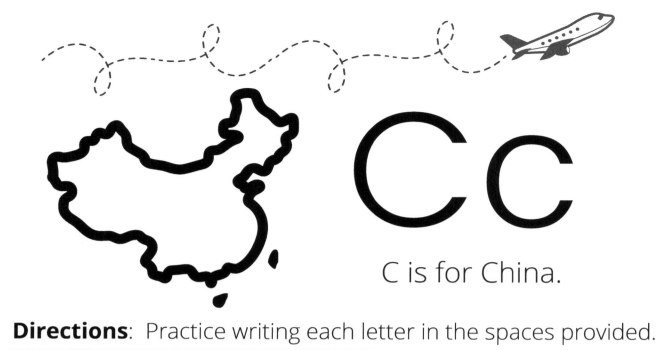

Cc

C is for China.

Directions: Practice writing each letter in the spaces provided.

Directions: Practice writing the letter in each space provided.

C C C C C

Directions: Practice writing the letter in each space provided.

C C C C C C

Denmark

Denmark is a Scandinavian country located on the continent of Europe. The people of Denmark speak Danish and Copenhagen is the country's capital city. Known for its rich Viking history, Denmark has waterways and rivers that flow throughout the land. The mute swan is Denmark's national animal.

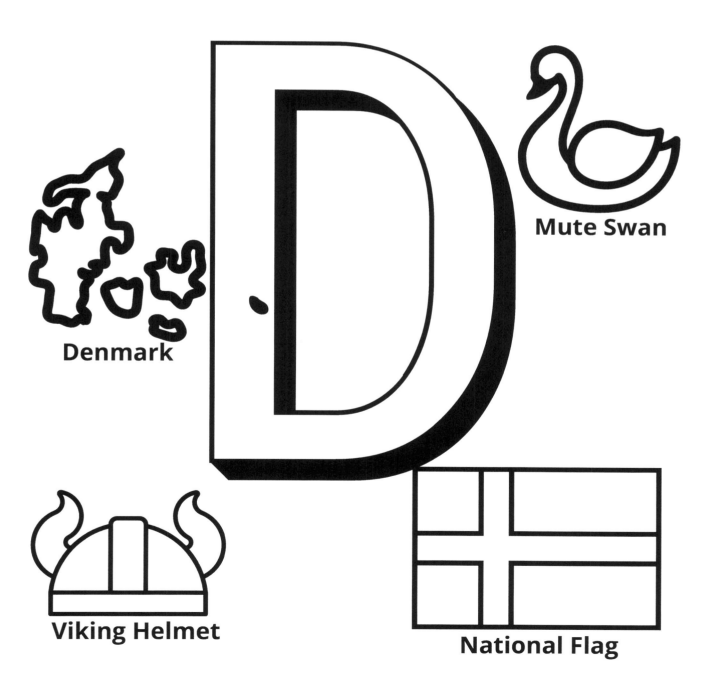

Denmark

Mute Swan

Viking Helmet

National Flag

Dd

D is for Denmark.

Directions: Practice writing each letter in the spaces provided.

Directions: Practice writing the letter in each space provided.

D D D D D

Directions: Practice writing the letter in each space provided.

d d d d d

Egypt

Egypt is located in Northern Africa and its capital city is Cairo. The people of Egypt speak Arabic. This land has a renowned history of ancient Pharaohs, vast desert lands, and historic pyramids – including the Great Pyramids of Giza.

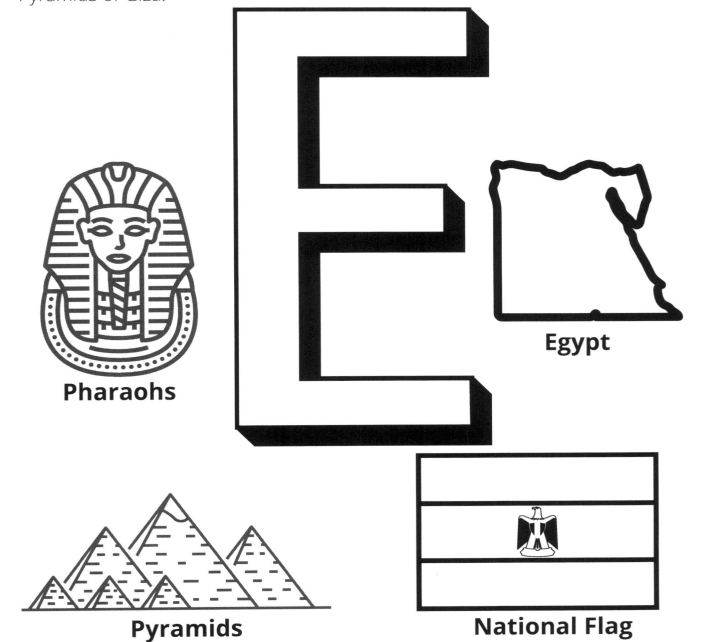

Pharaohs

Egypt

Pyramids

National Flag

Ee

E is for Egypt.

Directions: Practice writing each letter in the spaces provided.

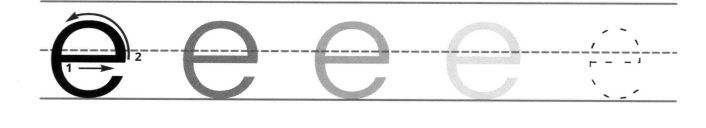

19

Directions: Practice writing the letter in each space provided.

E E E E E

20

Directions: Practice writing the letter in each space provided.

e e e e

France

France is the largest country in Western Europe and its capitol city is Paris. The country's national language is French. A beautiful land, France is well-known for its popular landmarks including the Eiffel Tower, the Louvre Museum, and several historic cathedrals.

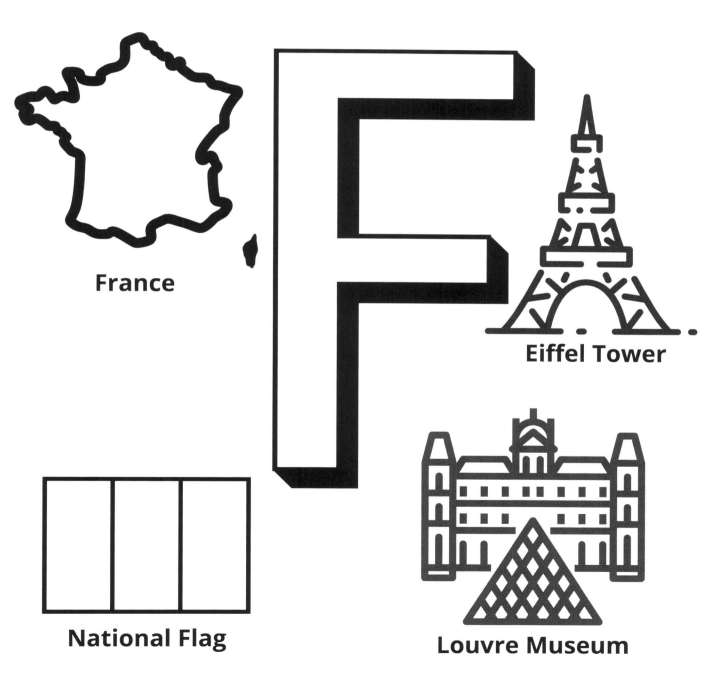

France

Eiffel Tower

National Flag

Louvre Museum

Ff

F is for France.

Directions: Practice writing each letter in the spaces provided.

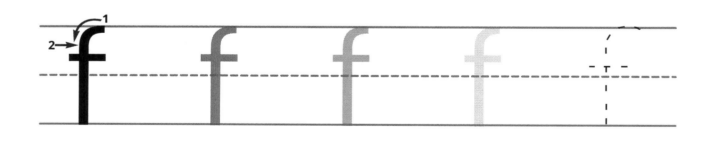

Directions: Practice writing the letter in each space provided.

F F F F F

24

Directions: Practice writing the letter in each space provided.

f f f f f

Germany

Germany is a Western European country where the people speak German. Germany's capitol city, Berlin, is also the country's largest city. This country is the birthplace of famous composers Bach and Beethoven. The country is also well-known for its vast forestlands and wildlife – including the wildcat.

Germany

Wildcat

Beethoven

National Flag

Gg

G is for Germany.

Directions: Practice writing each letter in the spaces provided.

27

Directions: Practice writing the letter in each space provided.

G G G G G

Directions: Practice writing the letter in each space provided.

g g g g g

Haiti

Haiti is a beautiful island located between the Caribbean Sea and the North Atlantic Ocean. The country's capital city is Port-au-Prince. Haiti has two national languages, Creole and French. The country is known for its stunning beaches and exports goods like coffee, mangos, and sugarcane.

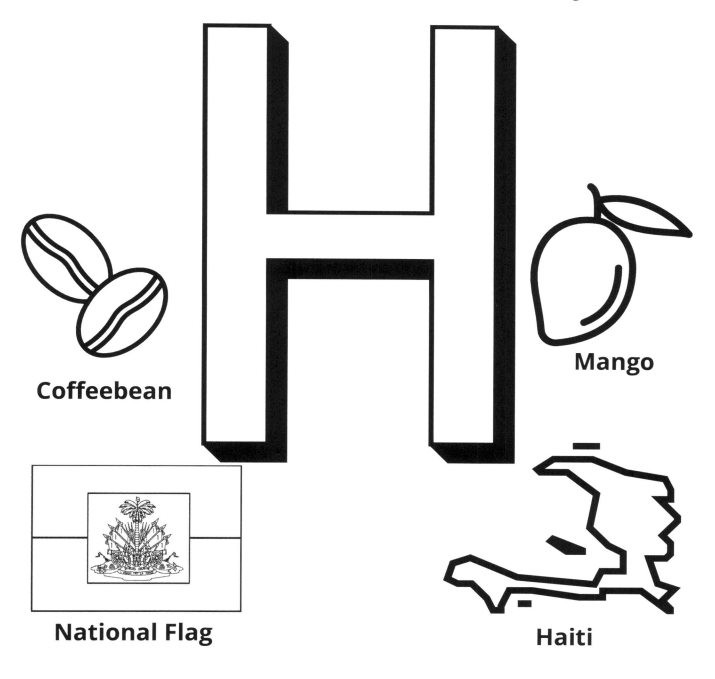

Coffeebean

Mango

National Flag

Haiti

Hh

H is for Haiti.

Directions: Practice writing each letter in the spaces provided.

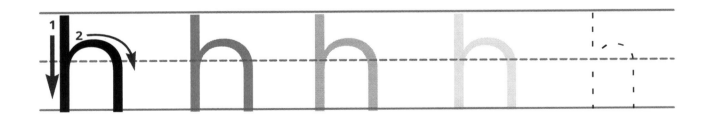

31

Directions: Practice writing the letter in each space provided.

H H H H H

Directions: Practice writing the letter in each space provided.

h h h h h

India

India is the third largest country in Asia and, has the second largest population in the world with 1.38 billion people. The country has 22 official languages including Hindi. India's national animal is the tiger and the country is home to the majestic Taj Mahal.

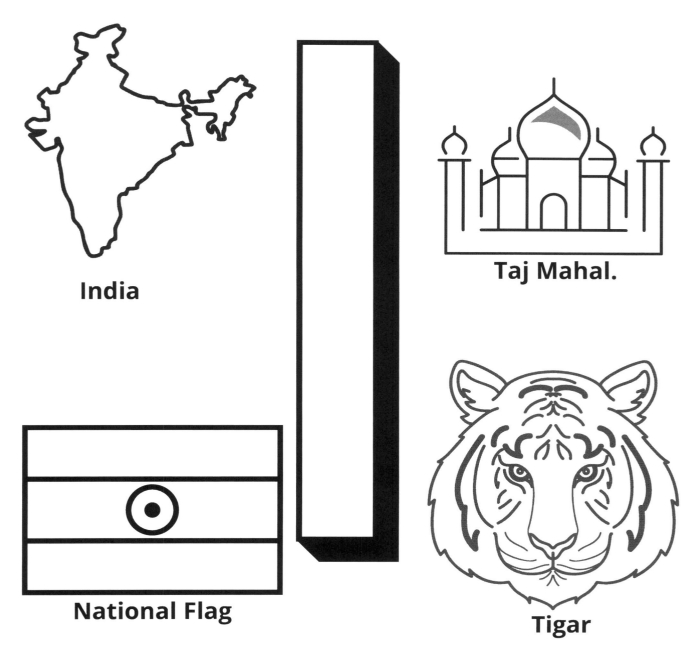

India

Taj Mahal.

National Flag

Tigar

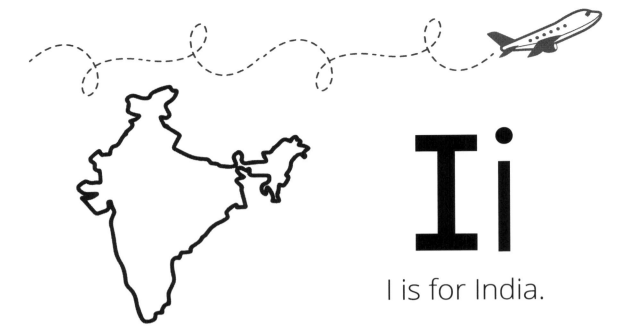

Ii

I is for India.

Directions: Practice writing each letter in the spaces provided.

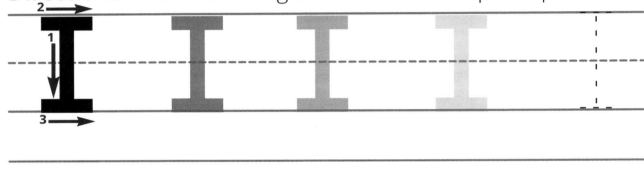

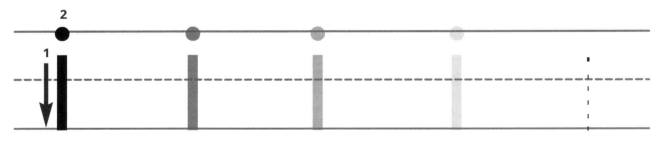

35

Directions: Practice writing the letter in each space provided.

I   I   I   I

Directions: Practice writing the letter in each space provided.

Japan

Japan is located off the eastern cost of Asia between the Pacific Ocean and Sea of Japan. The people of Japan speak Japanese and the capitol city is Tokyo. Japan is popularly known for Mount Fuji, a dormant volcano. The cherry blossom is Japan's national flower.

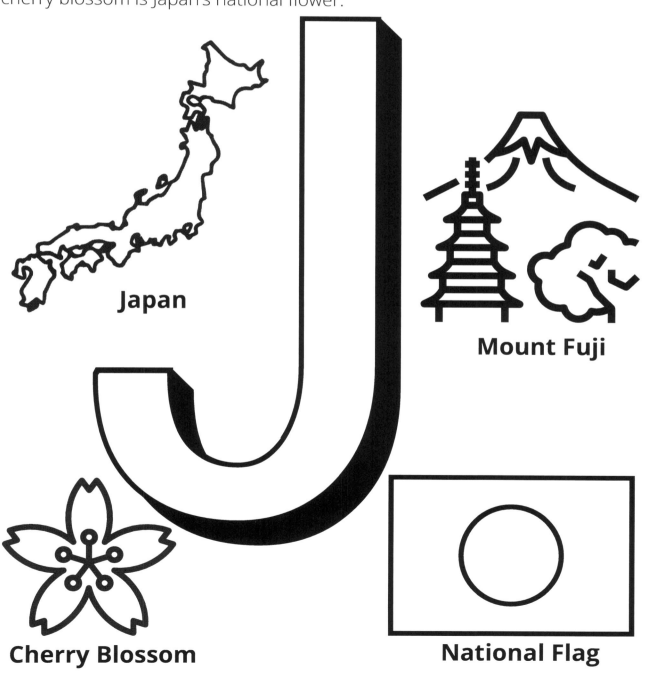

Japan

Mount Fuji

Cherry Blossom

National Flag

J j

J is for Japan.

Directions: Practice writing each letter in the spaces provided.

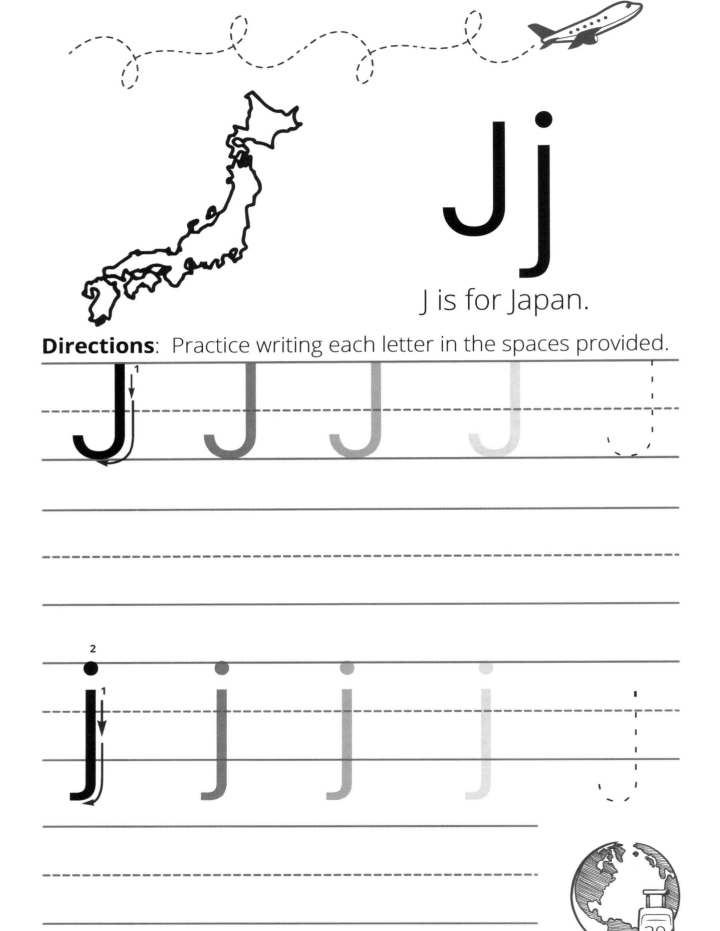

Directions: Practice writing the letter in each space provided.

J J J J J

40

Directions: Practice writing the letter in each space provided.

J J J J

Kenya

Kenya is located on the east coast of Africa. The country's coastline touches the Indian Ocean. Nairobi is the capital city of Kenya. Many languages are spoken in Kenya, but its national languages are Swahili and English. The land is known for its national parks filled with many animals like the mighty elephant. Kenya is also home to the world's fastest land animal, the cheetah.

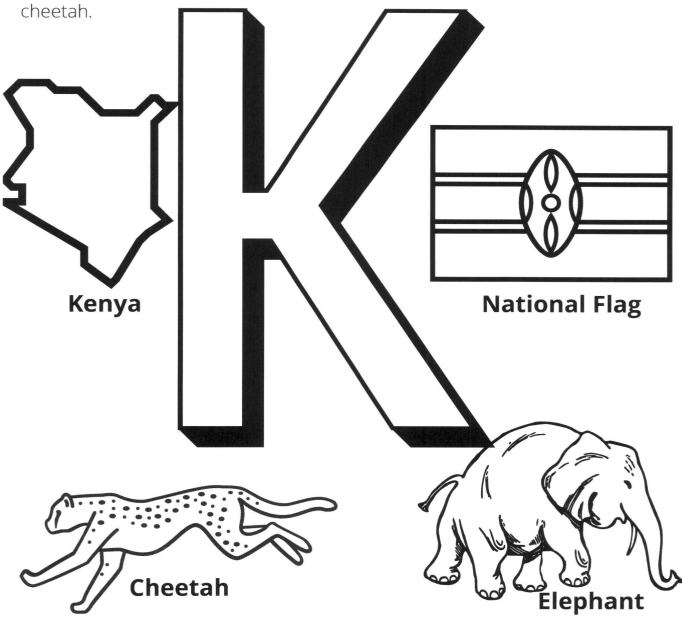

Kenya

National Flag

Cheetah

Elephant

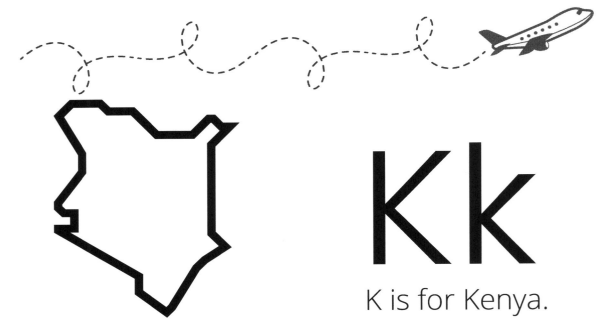

Kk

K is for Kenya.

Directions: Practice writing each letter in the spaces provided.

Directions: Practice writing the letter in each space provided.

K K K K K

44

Directions: Practice writing the letter in each space provided.

K K K K K

45

Liberia

Liberia is located on the west coastline of Africa. This land is known for beautiful savannahs and vast forestlands. Liberia is a diverse land with many different tribes of people. The capitol city of Liberia is Monrovia. English is the official language of Liberia; however, 29 other African languages are spoken throughout the land. Liberia's national animal is the Asiatic lion.

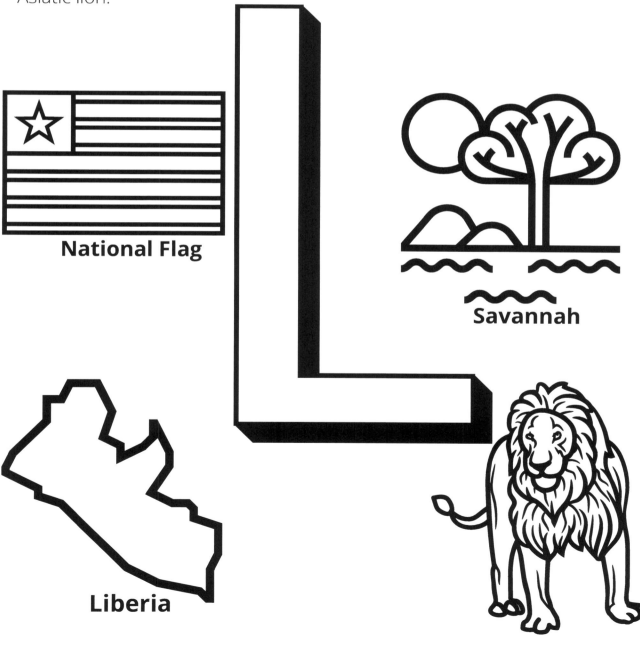

National Flag

Savannah

Liberia

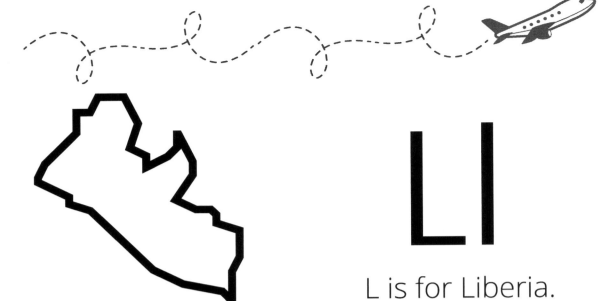

Ll

L is for Liberia.

Directions: Practice writing each letter in the spaces provided.

Directions: Practice writing the letter in each space provided.

1
2
L L L L

48

Directions: Practice writing the letter in each space provided.

1

Madagascar

The Republic of Madagascar is an island located off the southeastern coast of Africa. The fourth largest island in the world, Madagascar has two official languages Malagasy and French. The country's capital city is Antananarivo. Madagascar is popularly known for its lush rainforests and unique wildlife. Lemurs and tomato frogs are a couple of the unique wildlife native to Madagascar.

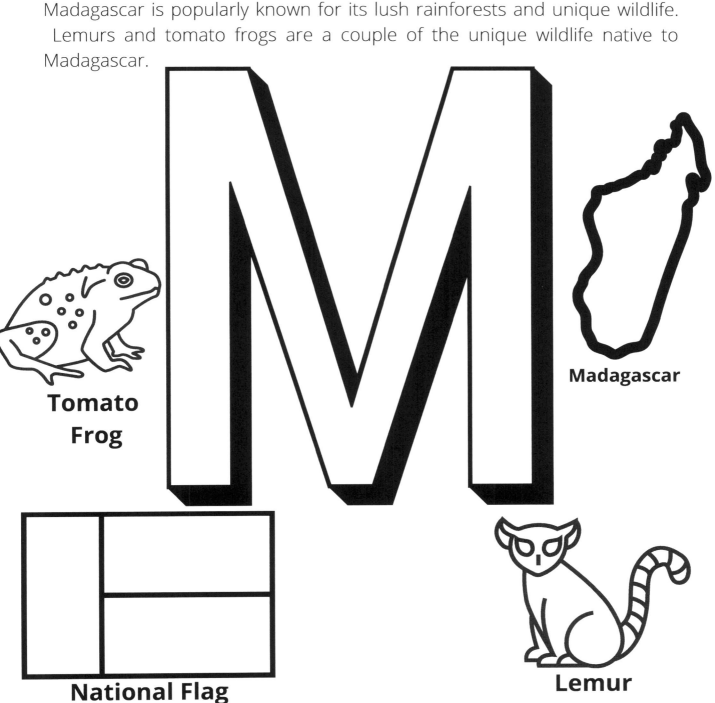

Tomato Frog

Madagascar

National Flag

Lemur

Mm

M is for Madagascar.

Directions: Practice writing each letter in the spaces provided.

M M M M M

m m m m m

51

Directions: Practice writing the letter in each space provided.

M M M M M M

Directions: Practice writing the letter in each space provided.

m m m m m

New Zealand

New Zealand is a group of islands located in the Pacific Ocean, off the southeast coast of Australia. The country's capital city is Wellington. There are three official languages: English, Māori, and New Zealand Sign Language. New Zealand is known for beautiful beaches, mountains, and wildlife including its national bird, the kiwi. The country is also known for its large population of sheep.

Sheep

New Zealand

National Flag

Kiwi

Nn

N is for New Zealand.

Directions: Practice writing each letter in the spaces provided.

Directions: Practice writing the letter in each space provided.

N N N N N N

Directions: Practice writing the letter in each space provided.

n n n n n

Oman

Oman is a country located in the Middle East and the country's capitol city is Muscat. This land is the oldest Arabian nation and the people of Oman speak Arabic. The land is known for its traditional and historic Arabian architecture, forts, and castles. The land is also home to the white Arabian oryx.

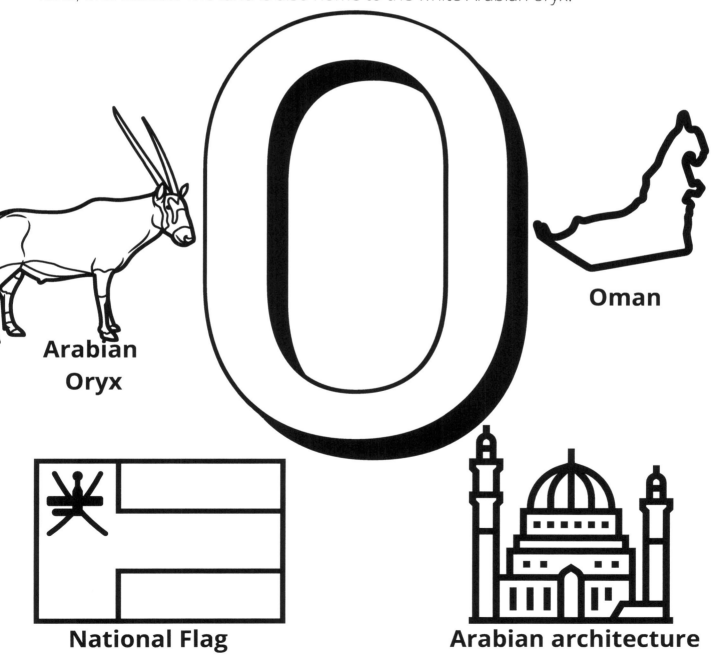

Arabian Oryx

Oman

National Flag

Arabian architecture

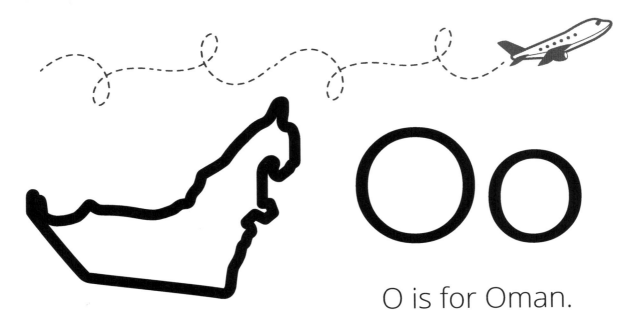

O is for Oman.

Directions: Practice writing each letter in the spaces provided.

Directions: Practice writing the letter in each space provided.

O O O O O

60

Directions: Practice writing the letter in each space provided.

O O O O ◯

61

Poland

The Republic of Poland is the largest country in Central Europe. Poland's capitol city is Warsaw and the national language is Polish. This land is known for historic museums, and castles. Poland is home to the world's largest brick castle, the Malbrok Castle. The White-tailed eagle is Poland's national animal.

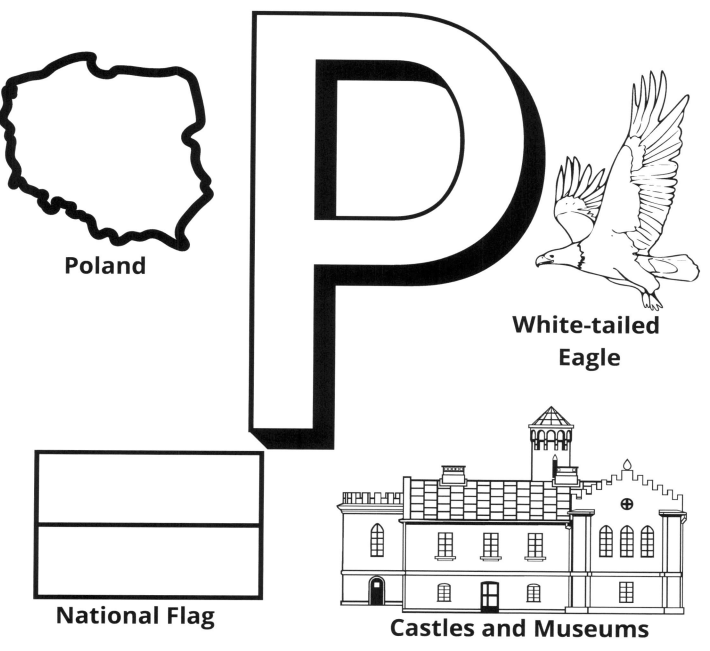

Poland

White-tailed Eagle

National Flag

Castles and Museums

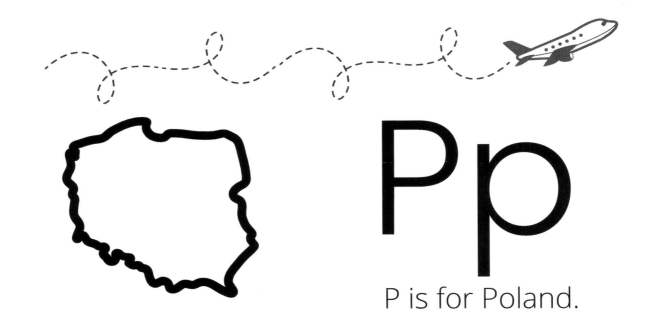

Pp

P is for Poland.

Directions: Practice writing each letter in the spaces provided.

P P P P P

p p p p p

Directions: Practice writing the letter in each space provided.

P P P P P P

Directions: Practice writing the letter in each space provided.

p p p p p

Qatar

Qatar is a country located in western Asia with vast desert lands. The country's capital city is Doha and the people of Qatar speak Arabic. The Arabian oryx is Qatar's national animal. This country has a wealth of natural minerals such as natural gas and oil.

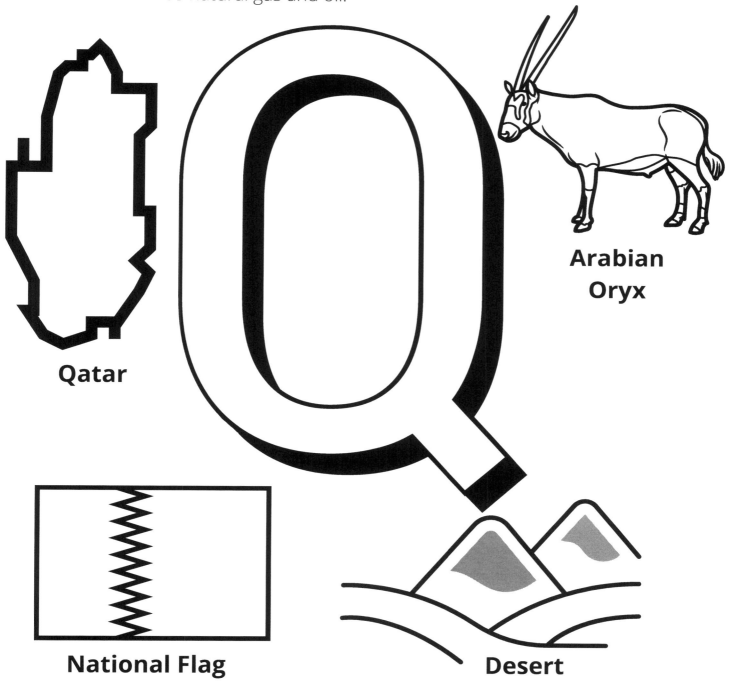

Qatar

Arabian Oryx

National Flag

Desert

Qq

Q is for Qatar.

Directions: Practice writing each letter in the spaces provided.

Directions: Practice writing the letter in each space provided.

Q Q Q Q Q

Directions: Practice writing the letter in each space provided.

q q q q q

Romania

Romania is an Eastern European country with beautiful, mountainous lands. The capitol city is Bucharest and the country's national language is Romanian. Black bears and the European Bison can be found in forests and throughout the country.

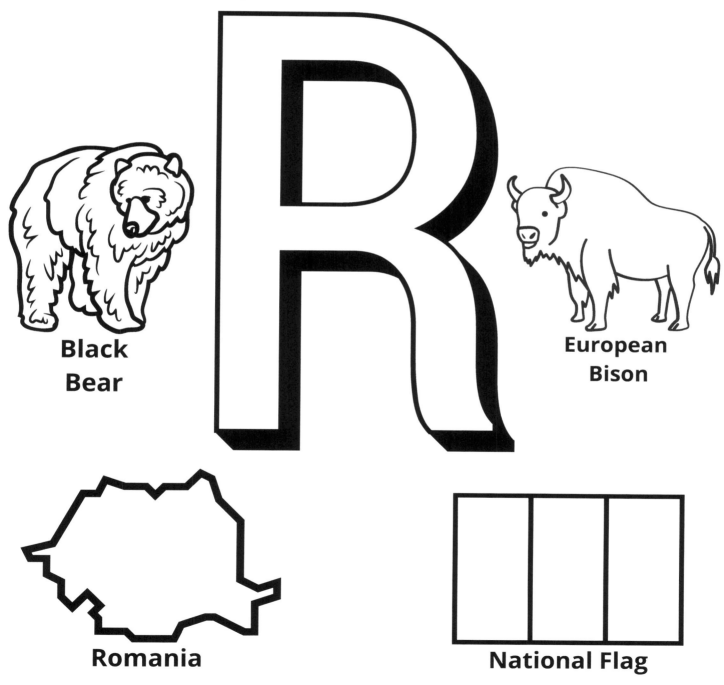

Black Bear

European Bison

Romania

National Flag

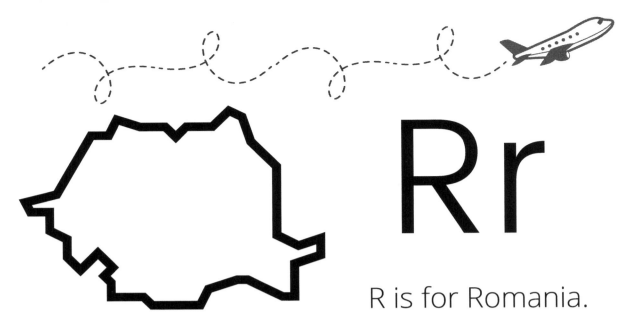

Rr

R is for Romania.

Directions: Practice writing each letter in the spaces provided.

R R R R R

r r r r r

Directions: Practice writing the letter in each space provided.

R R R R R R

Directions: Practice writing the letter in each space provided.

r r r r r

Singapore

The Republic of Singapore is located in southeast Asia. Singapore has four official languages: Malay, English, Mandarin Chinese, and Tamil. The country's national flower is the beautiful Miss Vanda Joaquim orchid. Singapore is home to incredible modern architecture including the Merlion Park and Helix Bridge. The lion is Singapore's national animal.

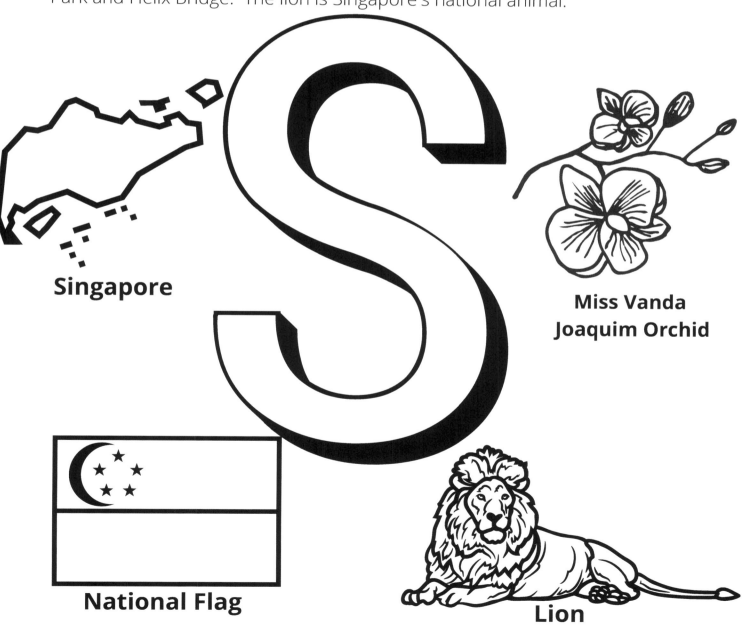

Singapore

Miss Vanda Joaquim Orchid

National Flag

Lion

Ss

S is for Singapore.

Directions: Practice writing each letter in the spaces provided.

S S S S S

S S S S S

Directions: Practice writing the letter in each space provided.

S S S S S

Directions: Practice writing the letter in each space provided.

S S S S S

Turkey

The Republic of Turkey, commonly called Turkey, is a peninsula that bridges Europe and Asia. Turkey's capitol city is Ankara. The people of Turkey speak Turkish. Turkey is surrounded by three seas: the Black Sea, the Mediterranean Sea, and the Aegean Sea. The national flower is the tulip which can be found all through the country. Turkey's national animal is the Grey wolf.

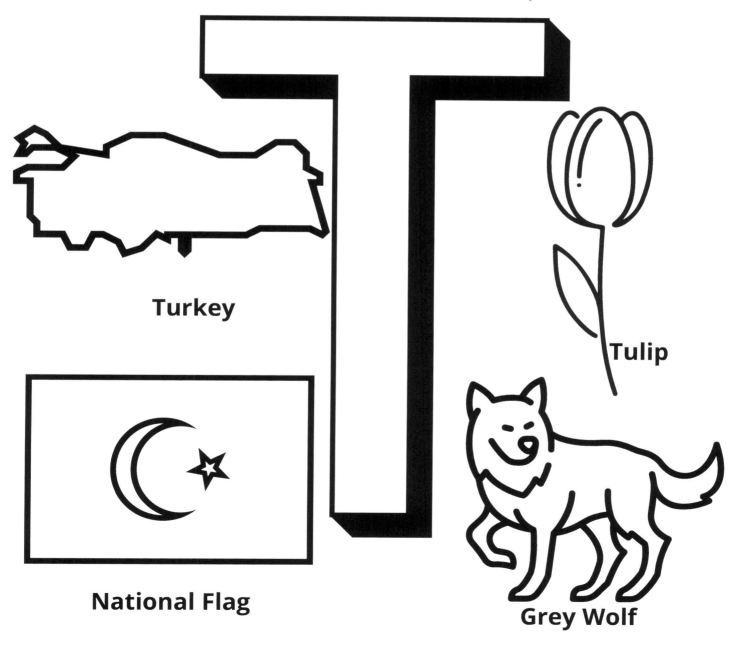

Turkey

Tulip

National Flag

Grey Wolf

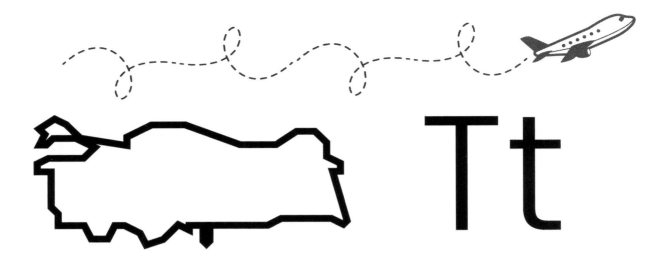

Tt

T is for Turkey.

Directions: Practice writing each letter in the spaces provided.

79

Directions: Practice writing the letter in each space provided.

2 → T   T   T   T
1 ↓

80

Directions: Practice writing the letter in each space provided.

t   t   t   t |

United Kingdom

The United Kingdom of Great Britain and Northern Ireland is commonly known as the UK. These lands are a group of islands located near the northwest coast of Europe. The UK includes England, Northern Ireland, Scotland, and Wales. Languages spoken in the UK include English, Welsh, and Irish just to name a few. Stonehenge and Buckingham Palace are famous landmarks located in the UK.. The UK's national animal is the lion.

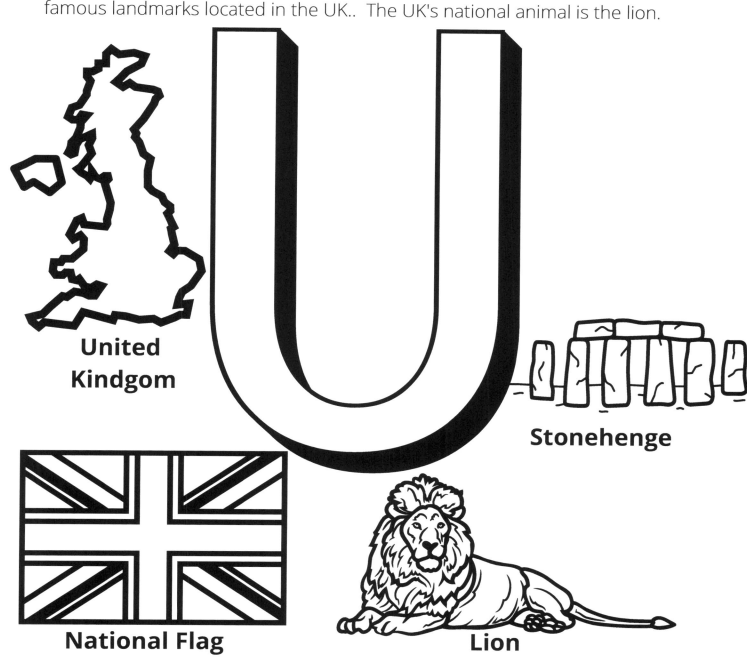

United Kindgom

Stonehenge

National Flag

Lion

Uu

U is for United Kingdom.

Directions: Practice writing the letter in the space provided.

Directions: Practice writing the letter in each space provided.

U U U U U

84

Directions: Practice writing the letter in each space provided.

U U U U U

Vietnam

Vietnam is located below China where it's eastern boarder touches the South China Sea. Vietnam is home to several stunning islands and inlets. The country's national flower is the lotus, and its national animal is the Water Buffalo. Vietnamese is the country's national language.

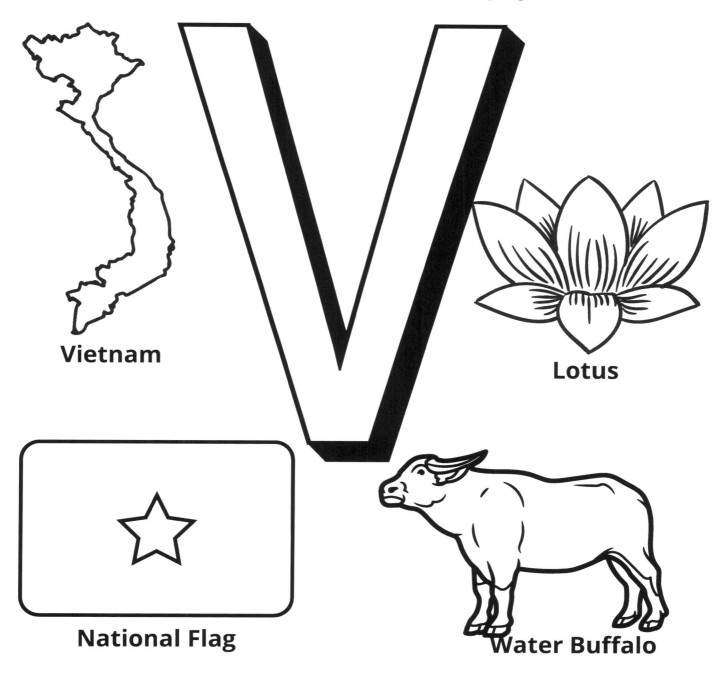

Vietnam

Lotus

National Flag

Water Buffalo

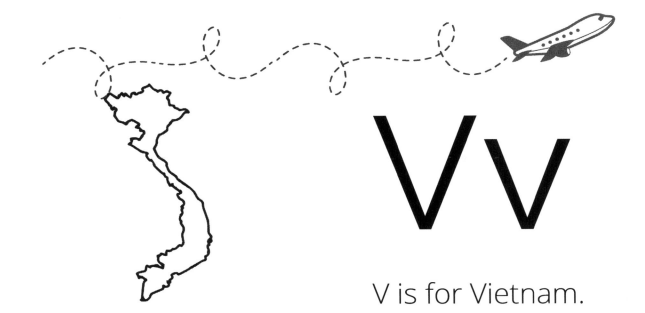

Vv

V is for Vietnam.

Directions: Practice writing each letter in the spaces provided.

87

Directions: Practice writing the letter in each space provided.

V V V V V V

88

Directions: Practice writing the letter in each space provided.

V V V V V

Wallis and Futuna

The Territory of Wallis and Futuna Islands are a collection of three volcanic islands. These lands are located in the South Pacific Ocean. As a French territory, the people of Wallis and Futuna speak French. The capital city is Matā'utu which is located on the island of Uvéa. The island of Uvéa has many coconut groves and pigs.

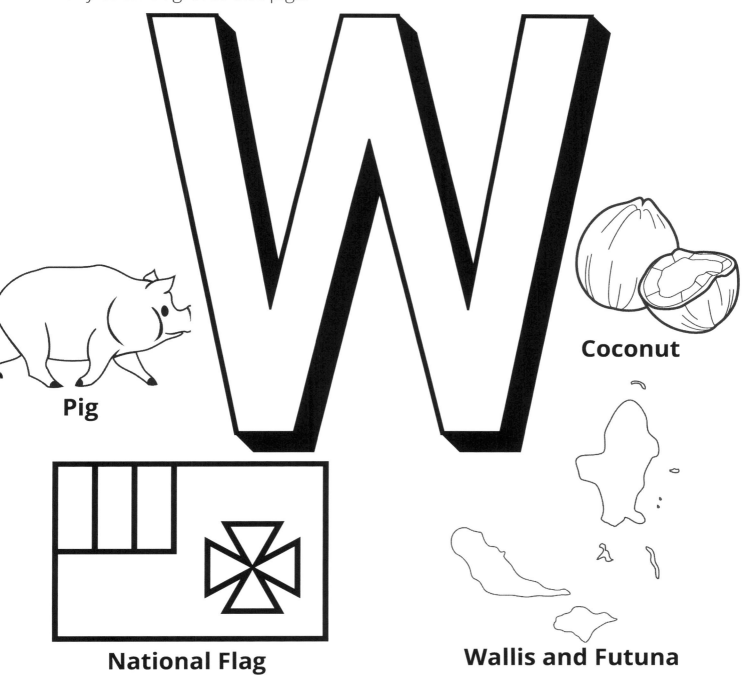

Pig

Coconut

National Flag

Wallis and Futuna

Ww

W is for Wallis and Futuna.

Directions: Practice writing each letter in the spaces provided.

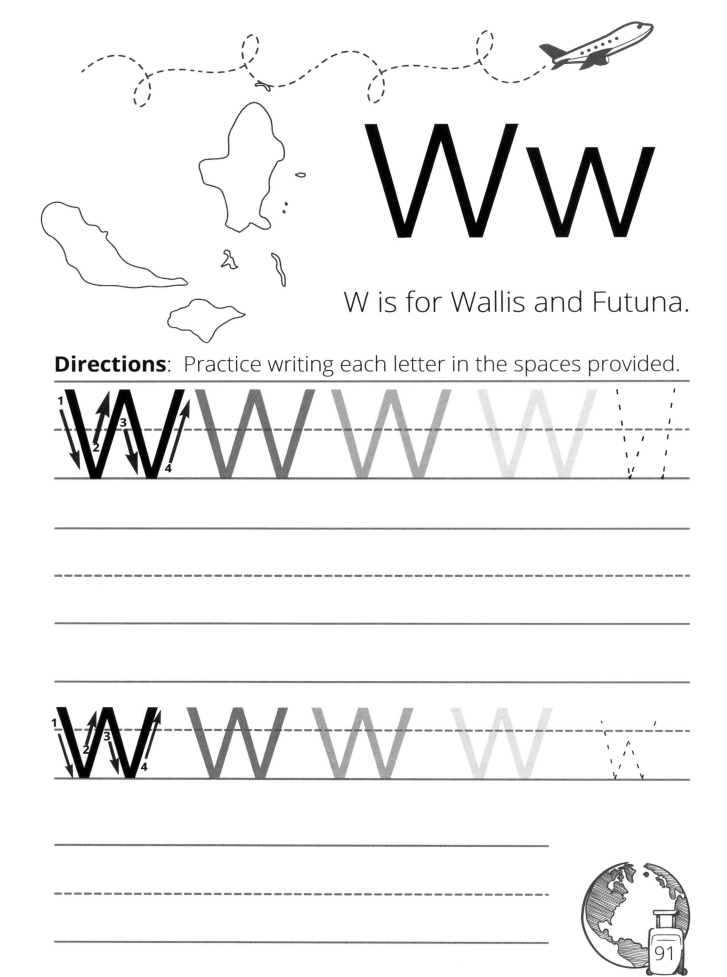

Directions: Practice writing the letter in each space provided.

W W W W W

Directions: Practice writing the letter in each space provided.

W W W W W

Xalapa

Xalapa is the capital city of the Mexican state, Veracruz. The city of Xalapa is the second-largest city in Veracruz. The people of Veracruz speak Orizaba Nahuatl, a Native American language spoken in southeastern Mexico. One of 32 Mexican states, Veracruz is located on the eastern coast of Mexico and touches the Gulf of Mexico. Iguanas are a common animal found in Veracruz.

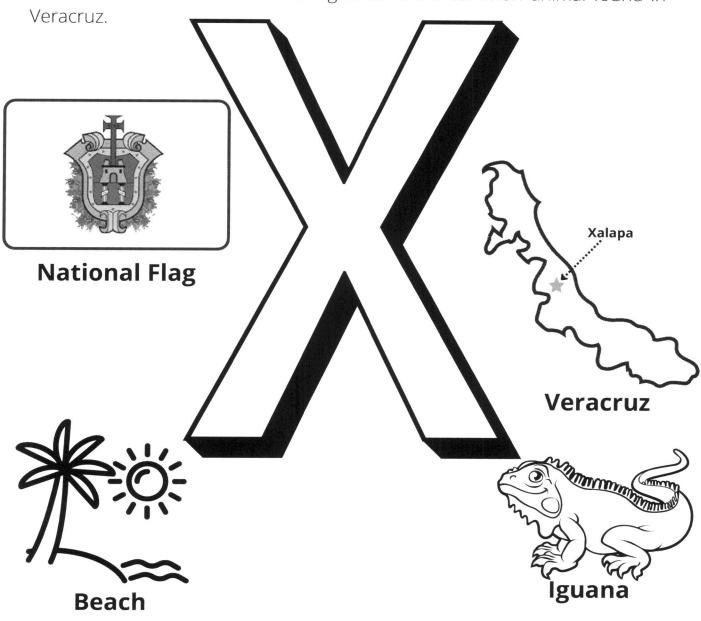

National Flag

Xalapa

Veracruz

Beach

Iguana

Xx

X is for
Xalapa, Veracruz (Mexico).

Directions: Practice writing each letter in the spaces provided.

¹X²   X   X   X   X

¹X²   X   X   X   X

95

Directions: Practice writing the letter in each space provided.

X X X X X

96

Directions: Practice writing the letter in each space provided.

X X X X X

Yemen

The Republic of Yemen is the second-largest country on the Arabian Peninsula in Western Asia. The people of Yemen are called Yemeni and the official language is Arabic. In early times, the country was known for its beauty land and wealth of natural resources including oil and resin extracts Frankincense, and myrrh. The Arabian leopard is Yemen's national animal.

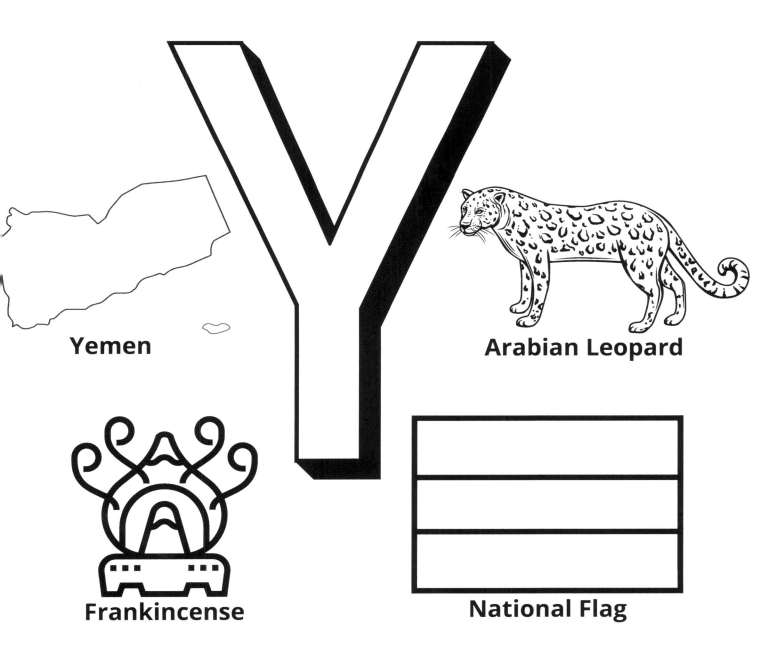

Yemen

Arabian Leopard

Frankincense

National Flag

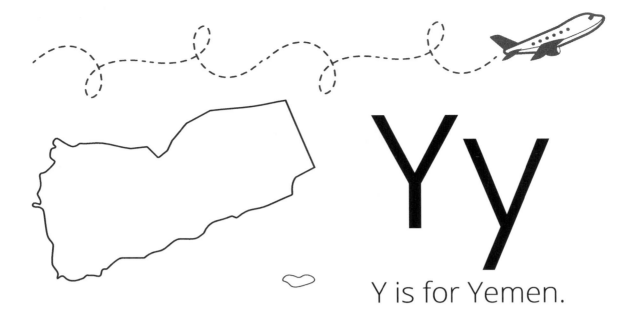

Y is for Yemen.

Directions: Practice writing each letter in the spaces provided.

Directions: Practice writing the letter in each space provided.

Y Y Y Y Y

Directions: Practice writing the letter in each space provided.

y y y y y

Zambia

The Republic of Zambia is located in Africa. Zambia has seven official languages: Bemba, Nyanja, Lozi, Tonga, Luvale, Lunda, and Kaonde. However, English is commonly used by the government and education. Zambia is home to Victoria Falls, the world's largest waterfalls. The country is also known for the unique umbrella-shaped dragon blood tree.

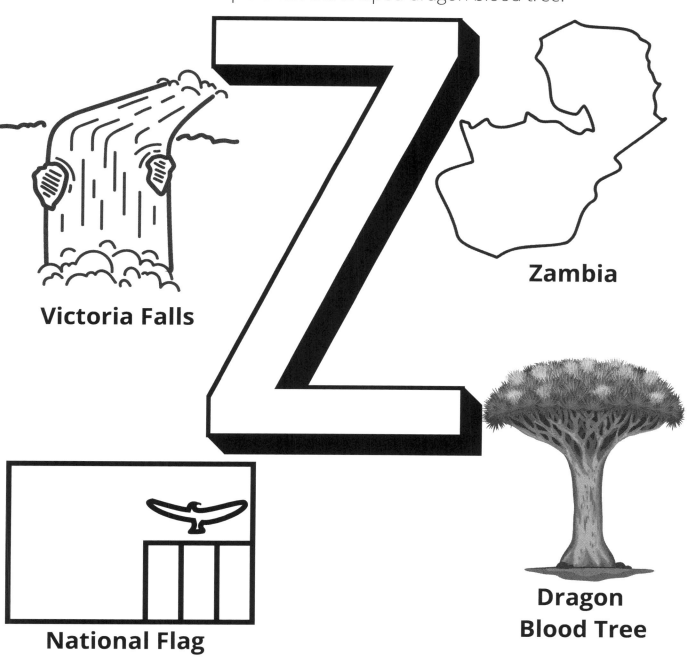

Victoria Falls

Zambia

National Flag

Dragon Blood Tree

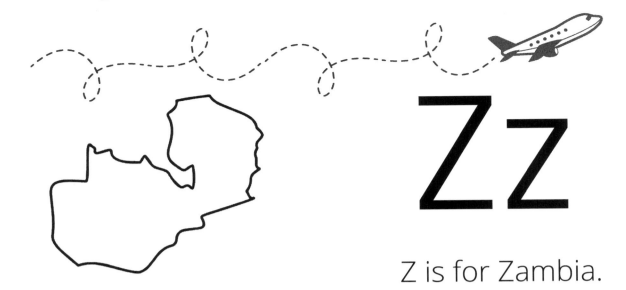

Zz

Z is for Zambia.

Directions: Practice writing each letter in the spaces provided.

Directions: Practice writing the letter in each space provided.

Z Z Z Z Z

Directions: Practice writing the letter in each space provided.

1→ Z 2
3→

Z   Z   Z   Z